A TRUE BOOK™

My United States

New Hampshire

NEL YOMTOV

Children's Press®
An Imprint of Scholastic Inc.

Content Consultant

James Wolfinger, PhD, Associate Dean and Professor
College of Education, DePaul University, Chicago, Illinois

Library of Congress Cataloging-in-Publication Data
Names: Yomtov, Nel, author.
Title: New Hampshire / by Nel Yomtov.
Description: New York, NY : Children's Press, an imprint of Scholastic Inc., 2018. | Series: A true book | Includes
   bibliographical references and index.
Identifiers: LCCN 2017051023 | ISBN 9780531235652 (library binding) | ISBN 9780531250846 (pbk.)
Subjects: LCSH: New Hampshire—Juvenile literature.
Classification: LCC F34.3 .Y66 2018 | DDC 974.2—dc23
LC record available at https://lccn.loc.gov/2017051023

**Front cover: Climbers on Mount
Washington's Boott Spur Trail**

Back cover: Bear cub

Welcome to New Hampshire
Find the Truth!

Everything you are about to read is true *except* for one of the sentences on this page.

Which one is **TRUE**?

T or F New Hampshire was the ninth state to join the United States of America.

T or F The bald eagle is the state bird of New Hampshire.

UNITED STATES

New Hampshire

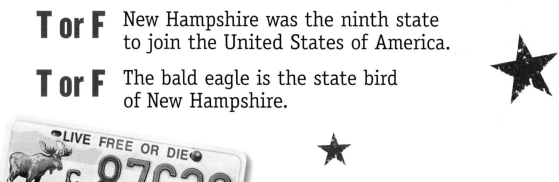

LIVE FREE OR DIE

C H 8763C

New HAMPSHIRE

Find the answers in this book.

3

Contents

THE BIG TRUTH!

What Represents New Hampshire?

Purple finch

Purple lilac

New Hampshire
Boat Museum

Cannon Mountain

5

This Is New Hampshire!

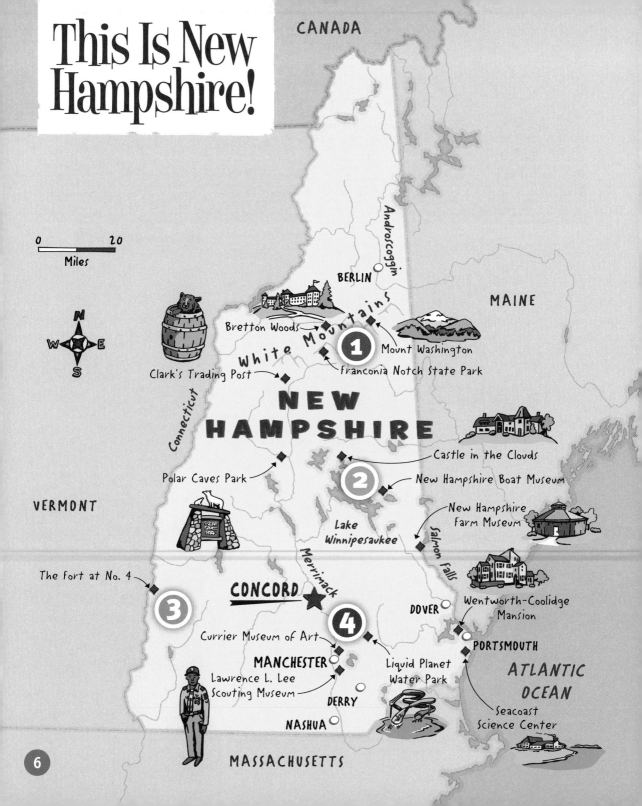

CANADA

MAINE

VERMONT

MASSACHUSETTS

ATLANTIC OCEAN

0   20
Miles

N
W   E
S

BERLIN

Androscoggin

Bretton Woods

White Mountains

Mount Washington

1

Franconia Notch State Park

Clark's Trading Post

Connecticut

NEW HAMPSHIRE

Castle in the Clouds

Polar Caves Park

New Hampshire Boat Museum

2

New Hampshire Farm Museum

Lake Winnipesaukee

Salmon Falls

Merrimack

The fort at No. 4

3

CONCORD

DOVER

Wentworth-Coolidge Mansion

4

Currier Museum of Art

PORTSMOUTH

MANCHESTER

Lawrence L. Lee Scouting Museum

Liquid Planet Water Park

DERRY

Seacoast Science Center

NASHUA

① Franconia Notch State Park

Located in the heart of White Mountain National Forest, this 6,700-acre (2,711-hectare) mountain pass is famous for its natural beauty. The park features an exciting ride that carries visitors 4,000 feet (1,219 meters) to the top of Cannon Mountain.

② New Hampshire Boat Museum

Founded in 1992, the museum is located in New Hampshire's scenic Lakes Region, near the town of Wolfeboro. The exhibits focus on the role that New Hampshire's waterways played in the development of the state.

③ The Fort at No. 4

Built by English settlers in the 1740s, this site is now a living history museum. Guides dress in period costumes to depict settlers and the town's military.

④ Currier Museum of Art

Art lovers can view the works of American and European painters, sculptors, and photographers at this world-class museum in Manchester. The museum also offers art classes.

The White Mountains cover about one-quarter of New Hampshire.

CHAPTER 1

Land and Wildlife

New Hampshire is nicknamed the Granite State for its many granite **quarries**. But the state offers much more than just durable construction materials. New Hampshire is rich in scenic beauty and history. Delightful lakes, woodlands, and mountains dot the landscape. As one of America's first **colonies**, New Hampshire's natural appeal is matched only by its long and proud history. For year-round fun and adventure, New Hampshire is the place to be!

A Diverse Landscape

New Hampshire is one of the six New England states. Shaped like a tall, narrow triangle, this small state ranks 46th in size among the states. The state of Maine and the Atlantic Ocean form the eastern border. To the south lies Massachusetts. Vermont forms the western border, and to the north is Canada. The geography of New Hampshire is divided into three main regions. They are the Coastal Lowlands, the New England Upland, and the White Mountains Region.

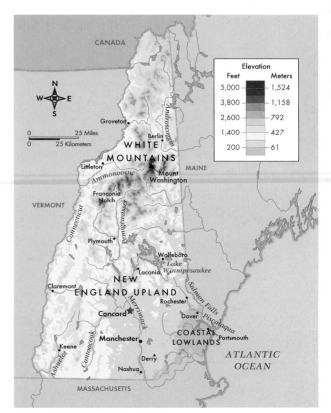

This map shows where the higher (red) and lower (green) areas are in New Hampshire.

The Loss of a State Symbol

For thousands of years, a strange and widely loved rock formation on Cannon Mountain, near Franconia Notch, gazed across New Hampshire's breathtaking landscape. Called the Old Man of the Mountain, the formation looked like the face of a tough, wise old man. But on May 3, 2003, the Old Man sadly disappeared. Centuries of **erosion** and harsh weather caused the massive stone face to collapse and fall into the valley below.

A crew works on the Old Man of the Mountain in the 1990s, before it crumbled.

11

Hampton Beach, New Hampshire's busiest coastal area, is home to many restaurants, shops, and other attractions.

The Coastal Lowlands make up the southeastern corner of New Hampshire. This region includes sandy beaches, wetlands, and the four islands that belong to the state. The New England Upland covers most of central and southern New Hampshire. Rolling hills, lakes, and most of the state's quarries are found here. The rugged White Mountains Region in the north features some of New England's tallest peaks. Deep, scenic valleys called notches were carved long ago by **glaciers**. Today, they are favorite spots for hikers.

Climate

New Hampshire generally experiences cool summers and very cold winters. The state's northern mountain region has the coldest winter temperatures. Daily lows in January average about 7 degrees Fahrenheit (–14 degrees Celsius). The average statewide temperature in July is a pleasant 82°F (28°C). Snowfall in some parts of the state is extremely heavy. Mount Washington, high in the White Mountains, receives an average of more than 280 inches (711 centimeters) of snow each winter.

MAXIMUM TEMPERATURE
106°F

MINIMUM TEMPERATURE
-50°F

Mount Washington is New Hampshire's highest peak.

In fall, many New Hampshire residents love to hike in wooded areas such as Crawford Notch State Park to see the changing leaves.

Plants

Forests cover more than 80 percent of New Hampshire. Hardwood trees such as oak, maple, and beech grow throughout the state's valleys. In the fall, the leaves of these trees turn spectacular shades of red, yellow, and orange. Evergreens such as pine, fir, and spruce also grow all over New Hampshire. In spring and early summer, wildflowers such as maiden pinks, azaleas, and purple lilacs brighten the woods.

Animals

New Hampshire is home to hundreds of animal species. Mammals such as black bears, white-tailed deer, lynxes, foxes, and coyotes roam the woodlands. Reptiles include American toads, red-spotted newts, and bullfrogs. Bald eagles, hawks, owls, meadowlarks, warblers, and sparrows soar through the skies. The Atlantic coastline is home to humpback whales, dolphins, cod, flounder, and mackerel. Bass, pickerel, trout, and pike swim in New Hampshire's freshwater areas.

A northern fin whale emerges above the surface of the Atlantic Ocean near New Hampshire to take a breath.

New Hampshire's capitol was built from granite blocks from local quarries.

DANIEL WEBSTER

CHAPTER 2

Government

The New Hampshire capitol in Concord was completed in 1819. It is built of smooth gray granite taken from quarries at the north end of town. The gold-covered metal eagle that now sits atop the capitol dome replaced the original painted wooden eagle. The New Hampshire capitol is the country's oldest original capitol where both houses of the legislature—the Senate and the House of Representatives—still meet.

Government at Work

New Hampshire's state **constitution** divides the government into three branches: executive, legislative, and judicial. The governor is the head of the executive branch. The legislative branch, called the General Court of New Hampshire, makes the state's laws. The judicial branch is a system of courts with several levels.

NEW HAMPSHIRE'S STATE GOVERNMENT

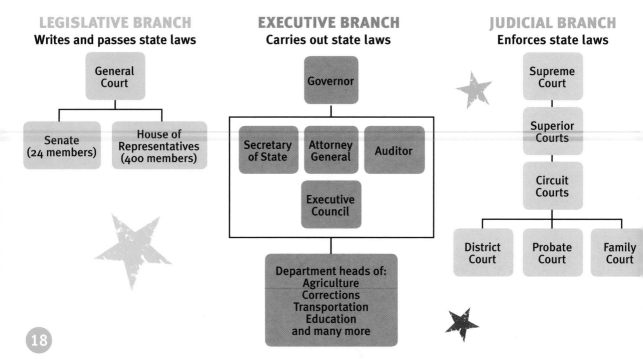

LEGISLATIVE BRANCH
Writes and passes state laws

- General Court
  - Senate (24 members)
  - House of Representatives (400 members)

EXECUTIVE BRANCH
Carries out state laws

- Governor
  - Secretary of State
  - Attorney General
  - Auditor
  - Executive Council
- Department heads of:
  Agriculture
  Corrections
  Transportation
  Education
  and many more

JUDICIAL BRANCH
Enforces state laws

- Supreme Court
- Superior Courts
- Circuit Courts
  - District Court
  - Probate Court
  - Family Court

Kelly Ayotte, one of New Hampshire's two U.S. senators, speaks at a town meeting in Goffstown.

Town Meetings

The town meeting is one of the oldest forms of local self-government in the United States. New Hampshire has been holding town meetings for about 380 years. Residents gather at a local hall to discuss and vote on the town's business, such as its budget. Historically, people were fined if they did not attend these important meetings. In the past, town meetings could last up to seven days in some parts of the state!

New Hampshire's National Role

Each state sends elected officials to represent it in the U.S. Congress. Like every state, New Hampshire has two senators. The U.S. House of Representatives relies on a state's population to determine its numbers. New Hampshire has two representatives in the House.

Every four years, states vote on the next U.S. president. Each state is granted a number of electoral votes based on its number of members in Congress. With two senators and two representatives, New Hampshire has four electoral votes.

2 senators and 2 representatives

4 electoral votes

With four electoral votes, New Hampshire's voice in national elections is below average.

The People of New Hampshire

Elected officials in New Hampshire represent a population with a range of interests, lifestyles, and backgrounds.

Ethnicity (2016 estimates)

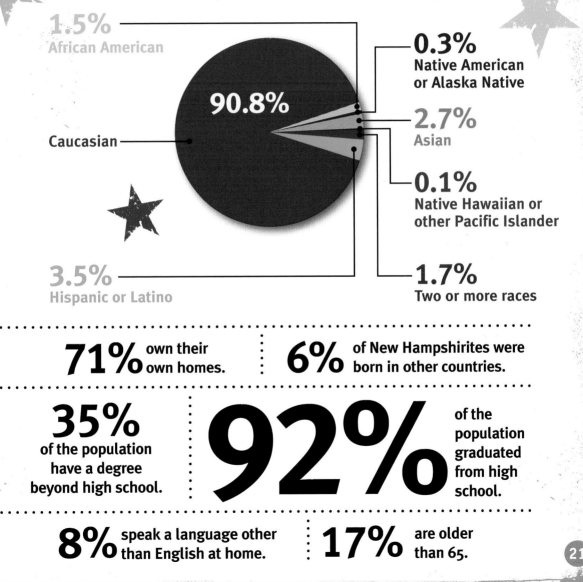

1.5%
African American

0.3%
Native American or Alaska Native

90.8%

2.7%
Asian

Caucasian

0.1%
Native Hawaiian or other Pacific Islander

3.5%
Hispanic or Latino

1.7%
Two or more races

71% own their own homes.

6% of New Hampshirites were born in other countries.

35% of the population have a degree beyond high school.

92% of the population graduated from high school.

8% speak a language other than English at home.

17% are older than 65.

What Represents New Hampshire?

States choose specific animals, plants, and objects to represent the values and characteristics of the land and its people. Find out why these symbols were chosen to represent New Hampshire or discover surprising curiosities about them.

Seal

New Hampshire's current state seal was created in 1931. It features the *Raleigh*, an early American warship that was built in Portsmouth. The seal also shows a rising sun and a circle of laurel leaves. The date 1776 honors the year the colonies declared their independence from Great Britain.

Flag

New Hampshire's state flag shows the state seal surrounded by laurel leaves and nine stars, which represent New Hampshire's place as the ninth state to join the Union. The flag was adopted in 1909 and changed slightly in 1931 to include the latest version of the state seal.

Purple Lilac

STATE FLOWER

Originally brought from England in the 1700s, the lilac has been the official state flower since 1919. A lilac bush can live for hundreds of years.

Purple Finch

STATE BIRD

Known for its pleasant "chur-lee" warble, this bird eats insects that can harm crops.

Chinook

STATE DOG

Affectionate and playful, the Chinook is the only dog breed developed in New Hampshire.

White-Tailed Deer

STATE ANIMAL

This beautiful animal can run up to 40 miles (64 kilometers) per hour and jump higher than 9 feet (3 m)!

Pumpkin

STATE FRUIT

The annual New Hampshire Pumpkin Festival features thousands of lit jack-o'-lanterns along with local food and music.

Brook Trout

STATE FISH

A member of the salmon family, brook trout thrive in clear, clean lakes, rivers, and ponds.

The New Hampshire Militia was a military force that played a major role in several Revolutionary War battles.

CHAPTER 3

History

Tens of thousands of years ago, present-day New Hampshire was covered by glaciers. As the ice melted or retreated northward, the first humans entered the region. Scientists believe the earliest people arrived around 12,000 years ago. They hunted large mammals such as mammoths, caribou, and musk ox. As the ice continued to disappear, warmer temperatures replaced the cold climate. People learned to make pottery and hunt for new game such as deer and moose using improved weapons.

Native Americans

By 1600 CE, thousands of **descendants** of the earlier people lived in the New Hampshire area. Most of them belonged to either the Abenakis in northern New Hampshire or the Pennacooks in southern New Hampshire. Both tribes were part of the Algonquian nation. They hunted and fished. They also gathered fruits, nuts, and berries in the woodlands. They grew corn, which they used to make fried or steamed corn cakes. Other crops included beans, squash, and pigweed, which could be eaten like spinach.

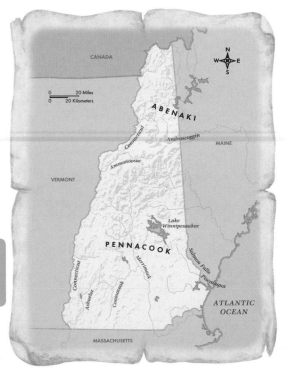

This map shows the two major tribes that lived in what is now New Hampshire before Europeans came.

Abenaki wigwams were made of bark, animal skins, and mats woven from reeds.

The Abenaki lived in small, round huts called wigwams and long, rectangular structures called longhouses. **Archaeologists** believe the Abenaki dwelled in both large villages and in smaller sites surrounded by their farm fields. They developed pottery for cooking and storage and made jewelry from colored stones. They generally lived in peace, but often fought the Iroquois people who lived to the west, in present-day upper New York State.

European Settlement

In 1614, English sea captain John Smith became one of the first Europeans to visit New Hampshire. Smith landed on the Isles of Shoals, the group of small islands in New Hampshire's Coastal Lowlands region. By the early 1620s, English settlers had established several small colonies near the Piscataqua River. For many years, the English and Native Americans traded peacefully. But as English settlers arrived in greater numbers, hostilities arose between the two groups.

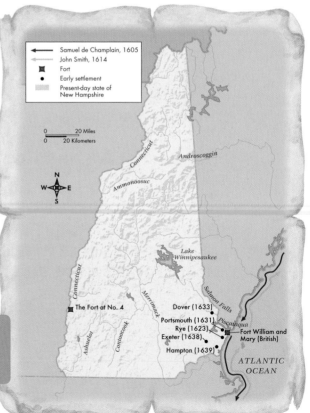

This map shows some of the early European settlements in what is now New Hampshire.

A military band formed from New Hampshire troops poses with their instruments at a camp in South Carolina during the Civil War (1861–1865).

In 1675, King Philip's War erupted. It was a bloody conflict between the colonists and Native Americans. During the yearlong war, many Native Americans were killed or sold into slavery. Others fled to Canada.

By 1775, the 13 American colonies were fighting Great Britain for their independence in the Revolutionary War. In 1776, New Hampshire became the first colony to adopt its own temporary constitution. After defeating Great Britain, the colonies created a constitution to govern their new nation.

A Rising State

On June 21, 1788, New Hampshire approved the U.S. Constitution and became the ninth state to join the United States. In 1808, Concord was made the state capital. New Hampshire grew rapidly. Farming and textile production became the state's major industries. During the Civil War (1861–1865), more than 35,000 New Hampshirites fought on the side of the Union.

Timeline of New Hampshire Events

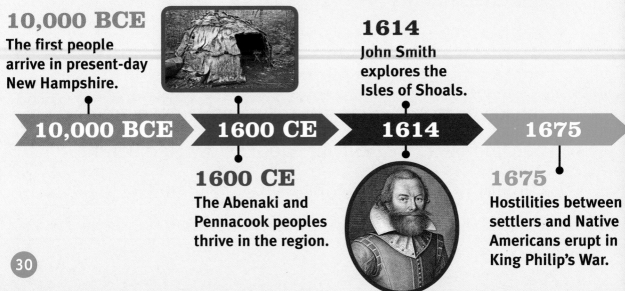

10,000 BCE
The first people arrive in present-day New Hampshire.

1614
John Smith explores the Isles of Shoals.

| 10,000 BCE | 1600 CE | 1614 | 1675 |

1600 CE
The Abenaki and Pennacook peoples thrive in the region.

1675
Hostilities between settlers and Native Americans erupt in King Philip's War.

The Twentieth Century

The Great Depression of the 1930s cost many New Hampshirites their jobs. A flood in 1936 destroyed roads and washed away homes. A terrible hurricane in 1938 caused widespread damage. During World War I (1914–1918) and World War II (1939–1945), shipyards along the New Hampshire coast manufactured submarines. By the 1950s, many people began to leave the state's cities to live in the **suburbs**.

June 21, 1788
New Hampshire becomes the country's ninth state.

2003
The famous Old Man of the Mountain rock formation collapses.

1775–1783 1788 1861–1865 2003

1775–1783
New Hampshire and other American colonies fight Great Britain in the Revolutionary War.

1861–1865
New Hampshire helps defeat the South in the Civil War.

New Hampshire Today

Like most states, New Hampshire suffered during the economic crisis of 2007–2008. The state lost thousands of jobs. State budget cuts badly affected hospitals, schools, and other public services. Some of the state's once-thriving paper mills were closed. In recent years, however, tourism, medical research, and high-tech industries have boosted the state's economy. As New Hampshirites continue to tackle new challenges, they remain confident they are heading in the right direction.

Lucia Ames Mead: Activist for Peace and Social Reform

Lucia True Ames Mead (1856–1936), born in Boscawen, devoted her life to peace, women's voting rights, and social reform. Mead believed that educators should not praise war to their students. In *What Young People Ought to Know About War and Peace* (1916), she wrote that war can be avoided and that there never has been a good war. Mead was an executive in the Woman's Peace Party and the Massachusetts Woman **Suffrage** Association.

CHAPTER 4

Culture

From thrilling outdoor activities to world-class museums and concert halls, New Hampshire is one of New England's most vibrant cultural centers. Residents and tourists enjoy plenty of opportunities to embrace the Granite State's arts and music scene, rich history, and joyous festivals and celebrations. As one former state slogan said, "You're Going to Love It Here!"

Dartmouth College's sports teams are known as the Big Green.

Sports and Recreation

College sports are a popular attraction in the Granite State. The University of New Hampshire and Dartmouth College have men's and women's teams in ice hockey, soccer, track and field, and other sports. The New Hampshire Fisher Cats are part of professional baseball's Toronto Blue Jays minor league system. Residents enjoy warm weather activities such as camping and hiking. In winter months, New Hampshirites delight in sledding, skating, and snowboarding.

Let's Meet at the Beach!

One of New Hampshire's most beloved celebrations is the Hampton Beach Seafood Festival, held each year in September. At New England's largest seaside event, more than 50 local restaurants offer delicacies such as clams, lobster, shrimp, barbecue, and mouthwatering desserts. Dozens of arts and crafts vendors display locally made items. Local bands entertain the huge crowds with the best in jazz, blues, R&B, and oldies. A dazzling fireworks display caps off the unforgettable weekend of fun.

Visitors enjoy local specialties at the 2017 Hampton Beach Seafood Festival.

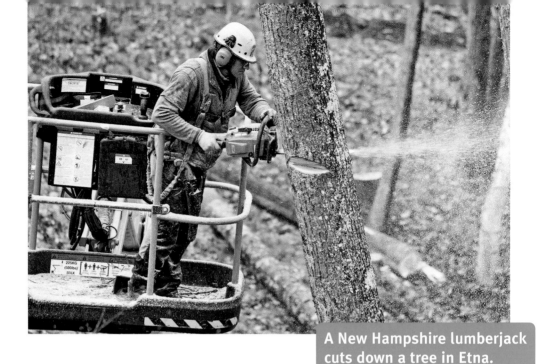

A New Hampshire lumberjack cuts down a tree in Etna.

Earning a Living

New Hampshire offers residents a wide range of employment opportunities. Apple growing, fishing, and dairy farming are among the state's leading industries. Many people work in tourism, banking and insurance, and healthcare. Others conduct high-tech research or manufacture computer parts and medical devices. New Hampshire's lumber industry employs about 16,000 people, while producing more than 50 kinds of wood products.

Adapting to a Changing Climate

In recent years, climate change has been leading to shorter winters in New Hampshire. The state's ski industry is responding to this change in exciting new ways. Some ski resort owners have begun to offer new activities to bring in guests outside of the winter ski season. These attractions include golf courses, mountain zip lines, and gravity coasters.

A train takes skiers to the top of a hill at the Loon Mountain ski area in Lincoln.

Hometown Eats

New Hampshire's farms and orchards grow flavorful apples, blueberries, sweet corn, and maple products. Residents also enjoy locally caught trout, bass, perch, lobsters, and clams. Shrimp corn chowder and creamy pumpkin soup are wintertime favorites.

New England Cranberry Relish

Ask an adult to help you!

Cranberries grow wild in New Hampshire, and the state's people often pick them to make this fall favorite.

Ingredients
1 small orange, unpeeled, seeded, and finely chopped
1 1/2 cups water
4 cups cranberries
1 cup sugar
Dash each of cinnamon, ginger, and cloves

Directions
Bring water to a boil. Cook orange in boiling water over medium heat until soft. Add all other ingredients. Cook, stirring often, until the berries start to pop open and the sauce thickens. Serve the relish while it's still warm or refrigerate it to enjoy a cool treat later!

You're Going to Love It Here!

You can spend a lifetime in New Hampshire and still not get to enjoy all the state's coolest attractions. For starters, visit the American Classic Arcade Museum in Laconia to learn about great video games of the past! Check

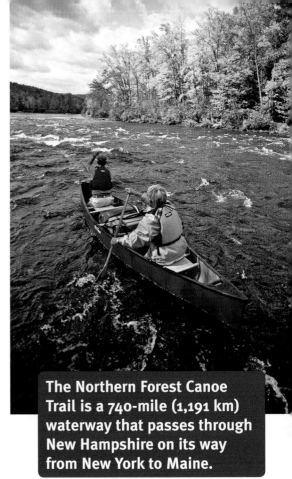

The Northern Forest Canoe Trail is a 740-mile (1,191 km) waterway that passes through New Hampshire on its way from New York to Maine.

out the Robert Frost Farm State Historic Site in Derry to see how one of America's most beloved poets lived. Stop by the Exeter UFO Festival and help locals celebrate the reported sighting of an alien spacecraft in 1965. In the Granite State, there is always something happening! ★

Famous People

Horace Greeley

(1811–1872) was a congressman from New York and the founder and editor of the *New York Tribune*. He popularized the phrase "Go West, young man" to encourage people seeking new opportunities in America. He was born in Amherst.

Augustus Saint-Gaudens

(1848–1907) was an Irish-born sculptor who created figures of Civil War generals and historic scenes. His summer home in Cornish is now a National Historic Site.

McDonald Brothers

The McDonald Brothers, Richard **(1909–1998)** (shown here) and Maurice **(1902–1971)**, were businessmen who founded the McDonald's chain of fast-food restaurants in California. They were born in Manchester.

Robert Frost

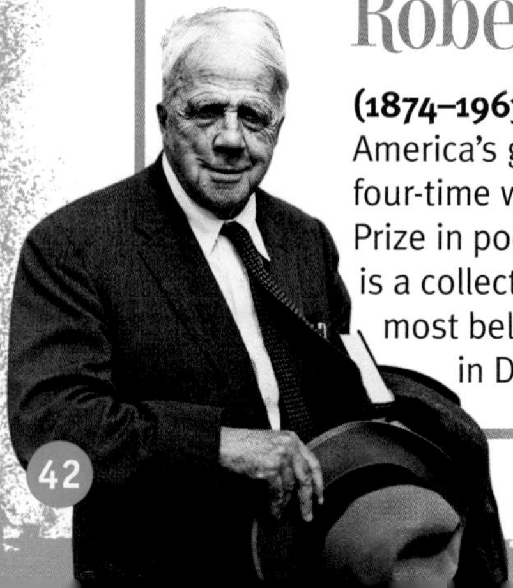

(1874–1963) was one of America's greatest poets and a four-time winner of the Pulitzer Prize in poetry. *New Hampshire* is a collection of many of his most beloved works. He lived in Derry and Franconia.

J. D. Salinger

(1919–2010), a longtime resident of Cornish, was a writer best known for the popular novel *The Catcher in the Rye*.

Penelope "Penny" Pitou

(1938–) was the first American skier to win a medal in the Olympics downhill racing event. In 1960, she won the silver medal at the Winter Olympics in Squaw Valley, California. She grew up in Center Harbor.

Alan Shepard Jr.

(1923–1998), born in Derry, was an astronaut. In 1961, he became the first American to fly into space. Later, he became the fifth person to walk on the moon.

Jodi Picoult

(1966–) is the best-selling author of more than 25 books, including novels, comic books, and short story collections. She lives in Hanover.

Sarah Silverman

(1970–) is a comedian, writer, and actor who has starred in such films as *Wreck-It Ralph* and *School of Rock*. She was born in Bedford and grew up in Manchester.

Seth Meyers

(1973–) is a writer, comedian, and television host best known for political humor. He grew up in Bedford.

Did You Know That...

Mount Washington in Coös County is the highest peak in the northeastern United States. It stands 6,288 feet (1,917 m) tall.

New Hampshire has the shortest coastline of any state bordering an ocean— about 18 miles (29 km).

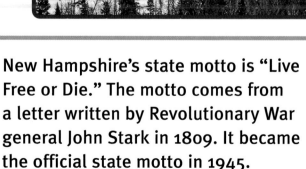

New Hampshire's state motto is "Live Free or Die." The motto comes from a letter written by Revolutionary War general John Stark in 1809. It became the official state motto in 1945.

The author of the poem "Mary Had a Little Lamb," Sarah Josepha Hale, was born in Newport.

The first free public library in the United States was established in Peterborough in 1833.

Franklin Pierce is the only U.S. president born in New Hampshire. He was the nation's 14th president.

The first potatoes grown in North America were planted in Derry in 1719.

Did you find the truth?

(T) New Hampshire was the ninth state to join the United States of America.

(F) The bald eagle is the state bird of New Hampshire.

Resources

Books

Cunningham, Kevin. *The New Hampshire Colony.* New York: Scholastic, 2011.

Rissman, Rebecca. *What's Great About New Hampshire?* Minneapolis: Lerner Publications, 2015.

Rozett, Louise (ed.). *Fast Facts About the 50 States: Plus Puerto Rico and Washington, D.C.* New York: Children's Press, 2010.

Waring, Kerry Jones, Terry Allan Hicks, and William McGeveran. *New Hampshire: The Granite State.* New York: Cavendish Square, 2016.

Visit this Scholastic website for more information on New Hampshire:

★ www.factsfornow.scholastic.com

Enter the keywords **New Hampshire**

Important Words

archaeologists (ahr-kee-AH-luh-jists) people who study the distant past, which often involves digging up old buildings, objects, and bones and examining them carefully

colonies (KAH-luh-neez) territories that have been settled by people from another country and are controlled by that country

constitution (kahn-stih-TOO-shuhn) the basic laws of a state or country that describe the rights of the people and the powers of the government

descendants (dih-SEN-duhnts) your descendants are your children, their children, and so on into the future

erosion (ih-ROH-zhuhn) the wearing away of something by water or wind

glaciers (GLAY-shurz) slow-moving masses of ice formed when snow falls and does not melt because the temperature remains below freezing

quarries (KWOR-eez) places where stone or sand is dug from the ground

suburbs (SUHB-urbz) areas on or close to the outer edge of a city

suffrage (SUHF-rij) the right to vote

Index

Page numbers in **bold** indicate illustrations.

About the Author

Nel Yomtov is an award-winning author who has written nonfiction books and graphic novels about American and world history, geography, science, mythology, sports, science, careers, and country studies. He is a frequent contributor to Scholastic book series.